HEART HABITS

Proven daily habits for a healthier heart

JAMES BONIFACE

Table of contents

INTRODUCTION

Although cancer deaths tend to get more attention, heart disease remains the leading cause of premature death in the United States and a health problem that affects both men and women. This can lower your risk of cardiovascular disease (heart disease and stroke). Let's take a look at some simple habits that can lower your risk of

cardiovascular disease
and heart attack.

CHAPTER ONE

Eat fish twice a week

Fish are an excellent source of protein, omega-3 fatty acids, and many vitamins and minerals "Eating at least two servings of fish per week may reduce the risk of heart disease." We recommend eating fish. However, it is important to avoid fish that are high in mercury. Shark; king

mackerel; tilefish
(goldfish); big eye tuna;
marlin; orange ruff, and
blue fish.

*Limit saturated and Trans
fats*

Saturated fats are found
in animal products such
as red meat and dairy
products, while Trans fats
are man-made fats
produced when
manufacturers add
hydrogen to vegetable

oils. It also increases the risk of heart disease and stroke by altering blood lipid levels.

To limit saturated fat intake:

- Eat less meat. Choose lean cuts (such as chicken breast trimmings), or trim the visible fat from the meat before cooking. Choose fish instead of red meat at least twice a week.

- Replace some of the meat in your diet with plant-based alternatives.

- Avoid processed meats such as sausages, bacon, and meats for lunch. Trans fats are found naturally in some foods such as meat and dairy products, but also in some processed foods. Trans fats, also called partially hydrogenated oils, are the "bad guys" in your blood. It increases the amount of LDL cholesterol and decreases the amount of "good" HDL cholesterol. Trans fats also increase inflammation in blood vessels, thereby contributing to arteriosclerosis (atherosclerosis). The U.S. Food and Drug Administration (FDA) banned Trans fats in food in 2018, but some still contain small amounts. Read the labels of packaged foods. If you see a partially hydrogenated oil on the ingredient list, it's best to avoid it as the product

contains a small
amount of Trans fat.

Fats Monounsaturated
fats are abundant in olive
oil, canola oil, peanut oil,
and avocado. These fats
lower "bad" LDL
cholesterol levels and
raise "good" HDL
cholesterol levels. They
are considered "good" fats
because they help lower

the risk of heart disease.
Monounsaturated fats
promote heart health by
lowering bad LDL
cholesterol and increasing
good HDL cholesterol.
Like extra virgin olive oil,
it also contains anti-
inflammatory compounds
that help reduce
inflammation in blood
vessels that lead to heart
disease. Replace
saturated fat in your diet

with monounsaturated
fat. For example, use
extra virgin olive oil
instead of butter.

*Choose whole grains over
refined grains*
Whole grains are a good
source of fiber, which
helps you feel fuller for
longer. They are also a
good source of B
vitamins, which are
important for energy
metabolism and heart

health. Avoid refined grains such as white bread and white flour. To create refined grains, manufacturers remove fiber and nutrients from whole grains. A lack of fiber spikes your blood sugar and isn't healthy for your heart. Soluble fiber, found in whole grains, also lowers cholesterol by binding to bile acids and transporting them out of the body before they are absorbed into the bloodstream. The American Heart Association recommends that most adults do not exceed 2,300 milligrams (about 1 teaspoon) per day.

CHAPTER TWO

Eat foods rich in potassium and

Magnesium

Potassium and magnesium are essential minerals for heart health. Potassium is abundant in fruits and vegetables, and magnesium is abundant in whole grains, nuts, and seeds. Potassium can lower blood pressure by reducing the load on arteries caused by sodium (salt). Magnesium has many benefits for heart health. Maintain healthy blood pressure and reduce insulin resistance, a precursor to type 2 diabetes and cardiovascular disease. Magnesium is also important for maintaining a healthy heart rhythm. If you have impaired kidney function or are taking a potassium-sparing diuretic for high blood pressure, talk to your doctor. In this case, they can advise you not to consume too much potassium. (BMI) is used to estimate whether your weight-to-height ratio is ideal. However, it does not take into account abdominal muscle mass or fat, which has a greater impact on the heart.

Maintaining a healthy weight is important for health, but so is maintaining a healthy waist size. Body mass index (BMI) is used to estimate whether your weight-to-height ratio is ideal. However, it does not take into account abdominal muscle mass or fat, which has a greater impact on heart disease than BMI. Don't just weigh yourself, measure your waist and be careful. Studies have shown that waist measurements of 40 inches or more in men and 35 inches or more in women are risk factors for cardiovascular disease.

Exercise most days of the week

One of the best ways to improve heart health is

regular exercise. The American Heart Association recommends at least 30 minutes of moderate-intensity aerobic activity (such as brisk walking or cycling) most days. If you are just starting to exercise, start slowly and gradually increasing the length and duration of your exercise. You can start with just 10 minutes of aerobic exercise each day and gradually increase the intensity and duration. Aerobic exercise also helps improve endurance. It makes more "random" movements. Get up, walk around and stretch so he doesn't sit for more than 30 minutes at a time. Sitting for long periods of time reduces insulin sensitivity and affects blood lipids in ways that

are detrimental to
cardiovascular health.

CHAPTER THREE

Conclusion

We hope these tips will help you live a healthier, happier life and prevent cardiovascular disease.

www.ingramcontent.com/pod-product-compliance
Lightning Source LLC
Chambersburg PA
CBHW060930130726
48001CB00006B/2510